Olivia
and the
Fairy Princesses

# Carrie Underwood

ABDO
Publishing Company

A Big Buddy Book
by **Sarah Tieck**

## VISIT US AT
**www.abdopublishing.com**

Published by ABDO Publishing Company, 8000 West 78th Street, Edina, Minnesota 55439.

Printed in the United States.

Coordinating Series Editor: Rochelle Baltzer
Contributing Editors: Heidi M.D. Elston, Megan M. Gunderson, Marcia Zappa
Graphic Design: Maria Hosley
Cover Photograph: AP Photo: Dan Steinberg
Interior Photographs/Illustrations: AP Photo: AP Photo (page 9), Henny Ray Abrams (page 29), Kevork Djansezian (pages 14, 25), Ed Gonser (page 21), The Oklahoman/Paul Hellstern (page 13), AP Images for Fox/Mark Mainz (page 19), Chris Pizzello (page 19), Chris Polk (page 19), John Russell (page 21), Mark J. Terrill (pages 19, 22), Norwich Bulletin/Khoi Ton (page 29); Getty Images: WireImage/Rick Diamond (page 27), WireImage/Ray Mickshaw (page 11), Tony R. Phipps (page 7), Kevin Winter (pages 5, 16).

### Library of Congress Cataloging-in-Publication Data

Tieck, Sarah, 1976-
 Carrie Underwood / Sarah Tieck.
    p. cm. -- (Big buddy biographies)
 Includes index.
 ISBN 978-1-60453-125-1
 1. Underwood, Carrie, 1983--Juvenile literature. 2. Singers--United States--Biography--Juvenile literature. I. Title.

ML3930.U53T54 2008
782.421642092--dc22
 [B]
                        2008010464

# Carrie Underwood

# Contents

# Music Star

Carrie Underwood is a famous singer. She is best known as a winner of *American Idol*. Since then, she has **released** albums and received awards for her music.

Carrie won *American Idol's* fourth season. Millions of people watch this television show and vote for their favorite singers.

## Where in the World?

Colorado | Kansas

Missouri

New Mexico

**OKLAHOMA**
Muskogee
Checotah

Arkansas

Texas

N
W E
S

# Family Ties

Carrie Marie Underwood was born on March 10, 1983, in Muskogee, Oklahoma. Her parents are Stephen and Carole Underwood. Carrie has two older sisters, Shanna and Stephanie.

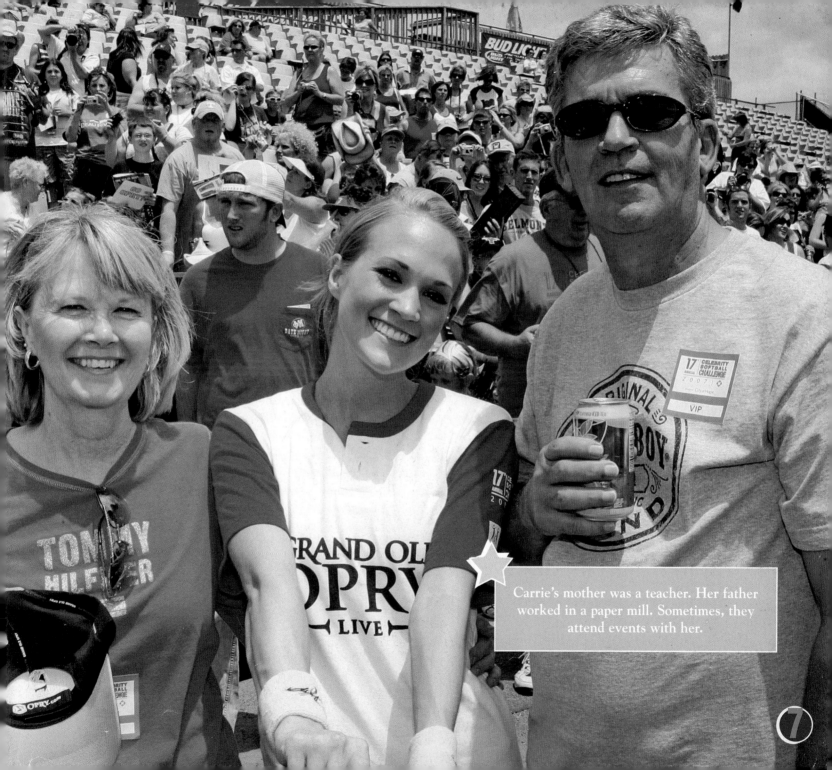

Carrie's mother was a teacher. Her father worked in a paper mill. Sometimes, they attend events with her.

Carrie grew up near Muskogee, Oklahoma. Her family lived on a farm in Checotah. Just 3,500 people live in this small town!

The Underwoods lived a quiet life in Checotah. They attended church and other local events.

Carrie has lots of fans in her hometown and around the world!

# Early Years

As a child, Carrie loved to sing. So, she began performing at church. Sometimes, she appeared in school plays and area talent shows. Friends and neighbors soon noticed Carrie's gift for music.

**Did you know...**

When she was 13, Carrie stopped eating meat. She made this decision because she loves animals.

When she was younger, Carrie dreamed of being a professional singer.

Carrie continued singing and performing throughout her high school years. When she graduated in 2001, she decided to go to college. Carrie attended Northeastern State University in Tahlequah, Oklahoma.

Carrie was a good student. She graduated with honors from both high school and college!

# Big Break

**Did you know...**

Flying to California for *American Idol* was Carrie's first airplane trip!

In 2004, Carrie heard about auditions for *American Idol*. She traveled to St. Louis, Missouri, for the first round of tryouts. The judges loved her!

Next, Carrie traveled to Hollywood, California. There, she had more auditions for *American Idol*. She was chosen to be a finalist on the show's fourth season!

One week on *American Idol*, Carrie *(above)* sang a rock song by Heart. The toughest judge, Simon Cowell *(left)*, loved it!

15

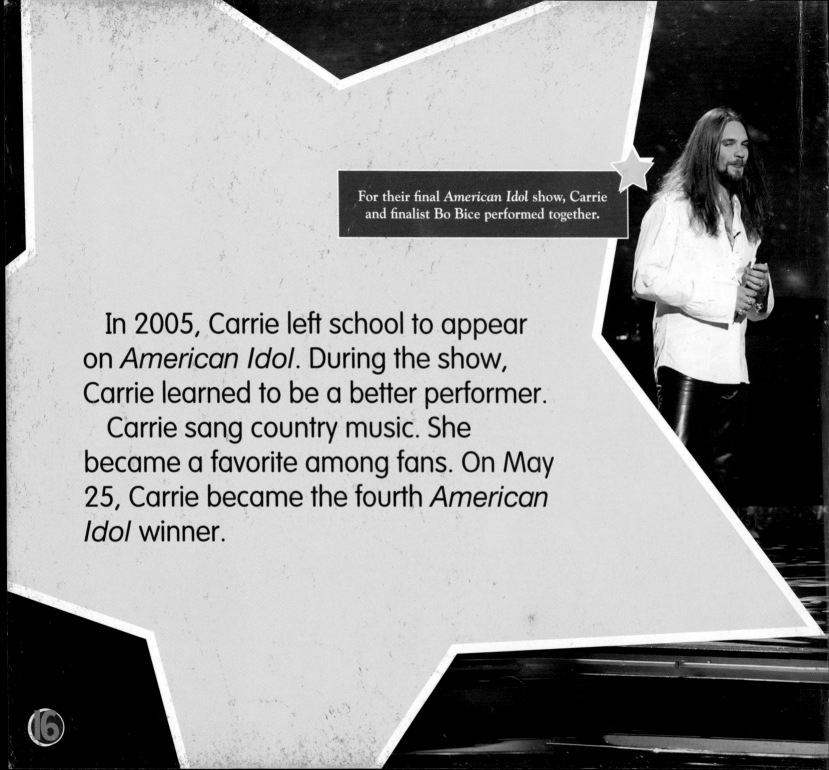

For their final *American Idol* show, Carrie and finalist Bo Bice performed together.

In 2005, Carrie left school to appear on *American Idol*. During the show, Carrie learned to be a better performer.

Carrie sang country music. She became a favorite among fans. On May 25, Carrie became the fourth *American Idol* winner.

# American Idol

*American Idol* is a popular television show. Each season, young people **compete** to be named the best U.S. singer.

Every year, thousands of people across the country **audition**. Judges choose a small group of finalists to perform.

Every week, each finalist sings and then viewers vote. The singer with the fewest votes leaves the show. Finally, one winner is chosen.

Kelly Clarkson, Jordin Sparks, and David Cook are three other *American Idol* winners.

Randy Jackson, Paula Abdul, and Simon Cowell are the show's judges. They remark on each performance before viewers vote.

Many singers have their picture taken for the public. This helps them and their music become better known.

# New Opportunities

After winning *American Idol,* Carrie began recording her first album. She also had more opportunities to perform. Carrie's dream of becoming a **professional** singer had come true!

After *American Idol*, Carrie used her fame to help people. She performed to raise money for the American Red Cross.

"Jesus, Take the Wheel" is one song on *Some Hearts*. Carrie performed this song at the Academy of Country Music Awards.

In November 2005, Carrie's first album was **released**. It is called *Some Hearts*. It features country pop songs. Millions of copies have sold!

## Did you know...

During *American Idol*, Carrie's fans called themselves Carrie's Care Bears.

# Awards and Honors

In 2007, Carrie won two Grammy Awards for her work. This was a big honor for her.

Carrie won another Grammy in 2008. She performed the winning song, "Before He Cheats," at the event. Since then, Carrie has been honored at the ACM Awards, the CMA Awards, and the CMT Music Awards.

**Did you know...**

*American Idol* winner Kelly Clarkson has also received Grammy Awards.

Carrie won her 2007 Grammy Awards for Best Female Country Performance and Best New Artist.

In May 2008, Carrie became a member of the Grand Ole Opry. This is an important honor for a country music singer.

The Grand Ole Opry is famous for its musical performances. They can be viewed live on stage or on television. Also, they can be heard on the radio. The Grand Ole Opry radio show began in 1925!

Garth Brooks gave Carrie her Opry Member Award.
Then, she and Vince Gill sang a song together.

# Buzz

Carrie's opportunities continue to grow and change. In 2007, she **released** her second album. It is called *Carnival Ride*. Like her first album, it is very popular.

Carrie continues performing her music in concerts and on television. In 2007 and 2008, she appeared on *Saturday Night Live*. Fans look forward to more music from Carrie Underwood!

In 2008, Carrie toured with country singer Keith Urban.

29

# Snapshot

★ **Name**: Carrie Marie Underwood

★ **Birthday**: March 10, 1983

★ **Birthplace**: Muskogee, Oklahoma

★ **Home**: Nashville, Tennessee

★ **Albums**: *Some Hearts, Carnival Ride*

★ **Toured with**: Kenny Chesney, Brad Paisley, Keith Urban

# Important Words

**audition** (aw-DIH-shuhn) to give a trial performance showcasing personal talent as a musician, a singer, a dancer, or an actor.

**competition** a contest between two or more persons or groups.

**Grammy Award** any of the more than 100 awards given each year by the National Academy of Recording Arts and Sciences. Grammy Awards honor the year's best accomplishments in music.

**professional** (pruh-FEHSH-nuhl) working for money rather than for pleasure.

**release** to make available to the public.

# Web Sites

To learn more about Carrie Underwood, visit ABDO Publishing Company on the World Wide Web. Web sites about Carrie Underwood are featured on our Book Links page. These links are routinely monitored and updated to provide the most current information available.

**www.abdopublishing.com**

# Index

3.9 AR Book level
0.5 Pts